60 MINUTE SEDER
COMPLETE PASSOVER HAGGADAH

M000009211

Contains all 15 parts of the Seder for a complete Passover experience.

"This spiritually uplifting Haggadah deserves a place at your Seder table."

Robert Kopman - best-selling author of 30minute-Seder™
"The Haggadah That Blends Brevity With Tradition"
& The 60minute-Seder™ Complete Passover Haggadah

★ Rabbinically approved

★ a complete Seder containing all 15 parts

★ includes after-dinner prayers

★ clear instruction so anyone can lead the Seder

★ larger easy-to-read format

★ gender-neutral text

★ beautiful illustrations keep everyone engaged

★ popular Seder songs included

"...guides you through all 15 parts of the Seder with just enough Hebrew, direction, and thought-provoking insight to guarantee a meaningful Passover experience for everyone."

Rabbi Bonnie Koppell - editor
First female Rabbi in the U.S. military

About the author

Robert Kopman has a long history of Jewish community involvement. He studied Jewish law and history in Jerusalem and is an expert on Passover Seder traditions. Originally from Brooklyn, New York, he currently resides with his wife and children in Arizona.

His first book, **30minute-Seder**™ "The Haggadah that Blends Brevity with Tradition," is the most popular reform/conservative Haggadah on the market today. As of this writing, it has sold more than 250,000 copies and is the #1 best-selling book in its class on Amazon.com.

30minute-Seder™

Author's note:
It's challenging to present all fifteen Seder parts in a concise manner while keeping the entire family engaged. Great care was taken to keep the after-dinner prayers brief, yet compelling, because many families don't come back to the table for the completion of the Seder. **60minute-Seder**™ meets that challenge easily and presents the story of Passover in an entertaining and spiritual way.

30minute-Seder™ was written for families that want the high points in a brief, yet spiritual format with a minimum of Hebrew. **60minute-Seder**™ has all of that; plus a compelling account of the ten plagues, and just enough Hebrew to satisfy the "maven" in your family.

I'd like to thank co-author and illustrator Bil Yanok, for his talents and many hours of work in creating such a unique and beautiful Haggadah. How he turned my words into such a stunning book and still kept it at an affordable price will forever remain a mystery to me.

- Robert Kopman

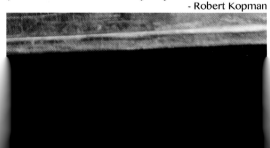

Introduction to
The Seder

In the Torah, God commands us to remove all chametz from our homes, eat unleavened bread (matzah), and most importantly, tell the story of Passover to the children every year. How we do that is open to interpretation and tradition.

One of Judaism's greatest scholars, Rabban Gamliel (gam-LEE-el), declared that the Seder is not complete unless we explain the meaning of the three symbols of Passover: Pesach, matzah, and maror. Jewish scholars say that the fifteen parts of the Seder should be mentioned in proper order. In fact, the word Seder means order.

This 60minute-Seder™ Haggadah (Haggadah means "the telling") is a guide to conducting a Passover Seder. Once a leader is chosen, feel free to add any cultural or family rituals, songs, or foods. Engage in discussions, enjoy the celebration, and take as much time as you like. Above all, feel gratitude for the freedoms we have today and enjoy your Seder!

Tip: When setting the table, keep flower arrangements and candles below eye level, so everyone can interact with each other ...especially the kids!

Preparing the Seder table

Seder Plate Ingredients
  Beitzah: hard-boiled, roasted egg
  Maror: red or white horseradish
  Chazeret: romaine lettuce
  Charoset: mixture of grated apples, nuts, and cinnamon, mixed
            with red wine
  Zeroa: a roasted lamb shank or chicken bone
  Karpas: parsley or similar spring vegetable

Haggadah for each participant
1 hard-boiled egg (peeled) for each participant
Bowls of salt water for dipping
Kosher for Passover wine and/or grape juice
Wine glasses
Matzah
Holiday or Shabbat candles
Water and a towel for ceremonial hand washing
Wine glass for Elijah
Water glass for Miriam (optional)
Pillows for reclining (optional)

> **TIP:** Many Jewish families serve gefilte fish, and chicken soup
> with matzah balls as appetizers. To avoid the cry of "When do
> we eat?" serve your appetizers before Seder begins.

We light
the candles...

We light the candles and recite the following prayer. Recite the words in parentheses if it's Friday night.

בָּרוּךְ אַתָּה יְיָ אֱלֹהֵינוּ מֶלֶךְ הָעוֹלָם, אֲשֶׁר קִדְּשָׁנוּ בְּמִצְוֹתָיו,
וְצִוָּנוּ לְהַדְלִיק נֵר שֶׁל (שַׁבָּת וְשֶׁל) יוֹם טוֹב:

Baruch Atah Adonai Eloheinu Melech ha'olam asher kid'shanu b'mitsvotav
v'tsivanu l'hadlik ner shel (Shabbat v'shel) Yom Tov.

Blessed are You, Adonai our God, Creator of the universe, Who makes us
holy with Your mitzvot, Who commanded us to light (Sabbath and) festival
candles.

בָּרוּךְ אַתָּה יְיָ אֱלֹהֵינוּ מֶלֶךְ הָעוֹלָם, שֶׁהֶחֱיָנוּ וְקִיְּמָנוּ וְהִגִּיעָנוּ
לַזְּמַן הַזֶּה:

Baruch Atah Adonai Eloheinu Melech ha'olam she'he'cheyanu v'kee'y'manu
v'hi'gee'anu la'zman hazeh.

Blessed are You, Adonai our God, Creator of the universe, Who gave us life,
sustained us, and enabled us to reach this season of joy.

"Seven days you shall eat unleavened bread;
on the very first day you shall remove leaven from your houses..."
Exodus 12:15

Removal of Chametz

God commands us to remove all chametz from our home. Chametz is defined as any food that's been leavened; especially the five grains of wheat, barley, spelt, rye, and oats.

`Everyone:` **Blessed are You, Adonai our God, Creator of the Universe, Who makes us holy with Your mitzvot, and Who commanded us concerning the removal of chametz.**

It's customary to make sure there's no trace of chametz. Some households empty the cupboards and clean the shelves of crumbs. One tradition is for the head of the household to search with a candle and wooden spoon for stray chametz. Any chametz found should be burned along with the spoon.

Seder participants should check for chametz on their clothing, in their pockets, and under their place settings.

And just to be sure... We say the following prayer:

`Everyone:` **Any chametz in my possession that I did or did not see, which I did or did not remove, shall be nullified and ownerless as the dust of the earth.**

THE SEDER

opening prayer

May all who are enslaved throughout the world, come to know freedom.
May all who are free, appreciate the blessings of abundance. May all of
us dwell in the house of God and give thanks for our good fortune as we
celebrate these rituals of Passover.

The Seder plate
contains the main symbols of Passover.

Beitzah
a roasted hard-boiled egg symbolizes the second sacrifice offered on Passover Eve

Maror
horseradish represents the bitter lives of the Jewish people as slaves of the Egyptians

Zeroa
a roasted shank bone symbolizes the Passover sacrificial offering

Chazeret
bitter lettuce also reminds us of the bitter lives of the Jews under the Egyptians

Charoset
a mortar-like mixture representing the slave-made bricks that built Egypt

Karpas
a spring vegetable (parsley) represents the celebration of the arrival of spring

The Seder has 15 parts, all of which must be performed in order. In fact...the word Seder means

"order."

קַדֵּשׁ   Kadaysh   (ka-DAYSH)

וּרְחַץ   Urchatz   (ur-CHATZ)

כַּרְפַּס   Karpas   (car-PAHS)

יַחַץ   Yachatz   (YA-chatz)

מַגִּיד   Maggid   (MA-geed)

רָחְצָה   Rachtzah   (rach-TZAH)

מוֹצִיא   Motzi   (MO-tzee)

מַצָּה   Matzah   (ma-TZAH)

מָרוֹר   Maror   (ma-ROHR)

כּוֹרֵךְ   Korech   (KO-rech)

שֻׁלְחָן עוֹרֵךְ   Shulchan Orech   (shuhl-CHAN o-RAYCH)

צָפוּן   Tzafun   (tsah-FOON)

בָּרֵךְ   Barech   (ba-RECH)

הַלֵּל   Hallel   (ha-LELL)

נִרְצָה   Nirtzah   (nir-TZAH)

Part 1

Kadaysh

Blessing over wine
(Kiddush)

We begin the Seder

Leader: Fill the wine glass of the person sitting next to you and all say:

בָּרוּךְ אַתָּה יְיָ, אֱלֹהֵינוּ מֶלֶךְ הָעוֹלָם, בּוֹרֵא פְּרִי הַגָּפֶן:

Baruch Atah Adonai Eloheinu melech ha'olam borei p'ri hagafen.

Blessed are You, Adonai our God, Creator of the universe, Who creates the fruit of the vine.

Blessed are You, Adonai our God, Creator of the universe, Who has chosen us from all nations, and made us holy with Your mitzvot.

And You, Adonai our God, have lovingly given us the Sabbath for rest, festivals for rejoicing, the spring Festival of Matzah, and a holy gathering in remembrance of the Exodus from Egypt.

Blessed are You, Adonai, Who makes holy; Shabbat, Israel, and the festive seasons.

Blessed are You, Adonai our God, Creator of the universe, Who keeps us alive and brings us together for this Seder.

Leader: Drink the first glass of wine while reclining, then refill your neighbor's cup. We recline to the left while drinking our wine as did the aristocracy in ancient times.

Part 2
Urchatz Washing of the Hands

instruction: Everyone (or just the leader) washes their hands at a sink, or at the Seder table with a water vessel and basin. No prayer is recited at this time.

Part 3
Karpas Vegetable

Everyone dips their vegetable into salt water and recites the following blessing:

בָּרוּךְ אַתָּה יְיָ, אֱלֹהֵינוּ מֶלֶךְ הָעוֹלָם, בּוֹרֵא פְּרִי הָאֲדָמָה:

Baruch Atah Adonai Eloheinu melech ha'olam borei p'ri ha'adamah.

Blessed are You, Adonai our God, Creator of the universe, Who creates the fruit of the earth.

Everyone now eats their vegetable.

Part 4
Yachatz Breaking of Middle Matzah

Leader: **instruction:** Uncover the matzah and break the middle matzah in two. Wrap the larger piece in a cloth (or Afikoman bag) for later use as the Afikoman. Place the smaller matzah piece between the sheets of whole matzot.

Place the wrapped Afikoman on your shoulder and say:

"In haste did we go out of Egypt."

Hide the Afikoman for the children to find after dinner. A reward is offered as a prize for finding it. An older more traditional ritual is for the children to steal the Afikoman. They may hold it for ransom or hide it for the head of the household to find, selling hints along the way.

"God heard their

and remembered the covenant with **Abraham, Isaac, and Jacob."**

Exodus 2:24

Participant: Once we were slaves to the Pharaoh in Egypt until God's mighty hand freed us. Had God not freed the Israelites, we might still be slaves in Egypt. So on this night we retell the story of Passover and give praise to God.

(Point to the matzah and say): This matzah is a symbol of affliction and poverty. The story of Passover tells us about the hardships and suffering that our ancestors endured. It reminds us of those who are in need today, so we say: "Whoever is hungry, come share our food; whoever is needy, come join us to help celebrate Passover!"

cries,

"We pray for those who are poor or oppressed...
and hope that the coming year will bring a better life for all."

Make sure the Passover story is told, and the significance of each Seder part is explained. If there are children present, encourage them to ask questions so they can understand the story better.

The Four

Leader: **instruction:** FIll the wine glass of the person sitting next to you. Don't drink it yet!

The youngest present then asks:

מַה נִּשְׁתַּנָּה הַלַּיְלָה הַזֶּה מִכָּל הַלֵּילוֹת?

Mah nishtanah halailah hazeh mikol haleilot?

Why is this night different from all other nights?

Leader:

This night is different in many ways. Which of these are the most meaningful to you?

The youngest present now asks:

שֶׁבְּכָל הַלֵּילוֹת אָנוּ אוֹכְלִין חָמֵץ וּמַצָּה הַלַּיְלָה הַזֶּה כֻּלּוֹ מַצָּה:

Sheh'b'chol haleilot anu ochlin chameits u'matzah, halaylah hazeh kulo matzah?

On all other nights we may eat chametz and matzah, but on this night, why only matzah?

שֶׁבְּכָל הַלֵּילוֹת אָנוּ אוֹכְלִין שְׁאָר יְרָקוֹת הַלַּיְלָה הַזֶּה מָרוֹר:

Sheh'b'chol haleilot anu ochlin sh'ar y'rakot, halaylah hazeh maror?

On all other nights we eat many vegetables, but on this night, why only maror?

שֶׁבְּכָל הַלֵּילוֹת אֵין אָנוּ מַטְבִּילִין אֲפִילוּ פַּעַם אֶחָת הַלַּיְלָה הַזֶּה שְׁתֵּי פְעָמִים:

Sheh'b'chol haleilot ein anu matbilin afilu pa'am echat, halaylah hazeh sh'tei f'amim?

On all other nights we don't dip even once, but on this night, why do we dip twice?

שֶׁבְּכָל הַלֵּילוֹת אָנוּ אוֹכְלִין בֵּין יוֹשְׁבִין וּבֵין מְסֻבִּין הַלַּיְלָה הַזֶּה כֻּלָּנוּ מְסֻבִּין:

Sheh'b'chol haleilot anu ochlin bein yoshvin uvein m'subin, halaylah hazeh kulanu m'subin?

On all other nights we eat either sitting up or reclining, but on this night, why do we all recline?

Questions

We begin to answer the questions...

"It was with a mighty hand that the Lord brought us out from Egypt, the house of bondage."

Exodus 13:14

Participant: On this night, we eat no chametz, only matzah. Not only because it is commanded by God in the Torah, but because it reminds us of our ancestors' haste in leaving Egypt. They had no time to let their dough rise and bake their bread properly; resulting in hard, flat crackers we call matzah.

On this night, we taste the bitterness of maror to remind us of the bitter lives of slavery our ancestors endured.

On this night, we dip twice: once with a vegetable into salt water to remind us of the tears shed by our ancestors, and once with maror into charoset, to remind us of the mortar used to lay the bricks of the Pharaoh's palaces.

On this night, we recline like ancient royalty while eating. We lean to the left emphasizing our feeling of freedom and good fortune.

The 4 C

Leader: The Torah uses the example of 4 children, each with unique abilities and needs, illustrating how children learn in different ways. This also reminds us of how, to varying degrees, we carry these traits through adulthood.

Children

The Simple Child   The Young Child

Take turns reading:

The wise child might be studious or innately smart. They pay attention to detail and enjoy learning. This child needs opportunities to discover the meaning of Passover on their own. Provide the tools to do so and explain why we tell the story of Passover every year, even if we already know it.

The wicked child is probably not really wicked, only rebellious. They'd rather be doing something else. Show them what they're missing by telling this compelling story. Encourage them to participate.

The simple child needs short, easy-to-understand explanations. You may have to provide the same explanation more than once. Keep things simple and teach them the general meaning of Passover without the details, until they're ready to learn more. Be patient, and they'll learn to appreciate the meaning of the holiday.

The young child is unable to ask a question or may not know what to ask. Explain the meaning of Passover in a way they can understand. Make them feel included in the festivities.

We Toast Our Endurance as a People

Throughout the ages we have endured. For not only has one risen against us to annihilate us, but in every generation they rise against us to annihilate us. But Adonai, the Holy One of Blessing, rescues us from their hand.

Put down the wine glass and uncover the matzot.

The Story of Passover

Take turns reading: We weren't always slaves in Egypt. The story of how we became slaves to the Pharaohs of Egypt and ultimately, how we were freed, is really the basis for the story of Passover. It's a part of history that belongs to all of us.

This story has been passed on from generation to generation, and tonight, especially if there are children present, you are helping to pass on an important tradition. By telling this story year after year, we ensure that we'll never forget our oppression or take our freedom for granted.

Many years ago, in the land of Egypt, Joseph, the son of Jacob and Rachel, was sold into slavery by his brothers. Joseph was skilled and intelligent, and soon became an official in the court of the Egyptian ruler, known as Pharaoh.

Joseph's specialty was interpreting dreams. Sometimes, he could even predict the future from a dream. One night, Pharaoh had a frightening dream of seven cows eating seven others, and seven heads of grain swallowing seven others. Not one of Pharaoh's advisors could interpret the dream. Pharaoh was reminded of Joseph's talent for predicting the future from dreams. Joseph foretold that Egypt would soon experience seven years of plenty followed by seven years of famine. Sure enough, his prediction came true.

Based on Joseph's advice, Pharaoh made preparations for the famine. The land of Egypt not only survived, it prospered. He was thankful for Joseph's wise advice, and so, when Joseph's family arrived in Egypt searching for food, they were invited to stay. The family lived in peace for many years and their descendants became known as Israelites.

Years later, after Joseph and all of his brothers had died, a new Pharaoh came to rule. The Pharaoh did not know Joseph and all that he had done for the Egyptians.

The Israelites were a very loving people and had many children. This alarmed the Pharaoh. His advisors told him that in the event of war, the Israelites might take the enemy's side and they would be outnumbered. Pharaoh decided that the best thing to do was drown any newborn Israelite boys in the river, limiting their population growth. The remaining Israelites were made slaves.

"Every baby boy born to an Israelite w

"And you shall explain to your children on that day, It is because of what the Lord did for me when I went free from Egypt."

Exodus 13:8

The Egyptian soldiers tried to kill the baby boys of the Israelites,

but many of them were saved by the brave Hebrew midwives and some kindhearted Egyptians.

Amram (AHM-rahm) and Yocheved (yo-CHEHV-ed), a Hebrew couple, were desperate to save the life of their child. To avoid detection from Egyptian soldiers, they placed the baby in a basket made of reed and pitch. Quietly they made their way to the banks of the Nile and placed him in the river amongst the reeds.

Their plan worked! The baby was discovered by Pharaoh's daughter, the princess. She was so smitten with the baby that she decided to adopt him. The princess named the baby Moses, be-cause it means "brought out from the water." Yocheved had a clever young daughter, Miriam, who was watching. "Do you need a nurse to feed and take care of Moses?", asked Miriam. "I know a very good one!" Miriam ran home, fetched her mother Yocheved, and brought her back to the Nile where the princess was waiting. Hired as nurse, Yocheved was able to raise her own son, where he got the best of everything in the palace.

As a baby, Moses loved to hang around Pharaoh and play. One day Moses pulled the Pharaoh's crown right off his head and placed it on his own! "Oh no !" Pharaoh's advisors gasped. "This is a very bad omen. We must put the boy to death immediately." Luckily for Moses, one advisor came up with a different plan. "Let's give him a choice between a gold vessel and a hot lump of coal. If Moses chooses the vessel, we'll know that he's clever and we'll have to kill him. If he chooses the hot coal, we'll know that he's not too bright and not a threat, and we can let him live." The other advisors happily agreed. Moses chose the hot coal and of course, he burnt his lips and tongue and was in great pain. "Well, Pharaoh, I guess he's not so smart after all, we'll let him live." said the advisors as they walked away laughing.

Years later when Moses was a young man still living in the palace, he witnessed an Egyptian taskmaster beating up an Israelite slave. Outraged, Moses beat the taskmaster to death. His murderous deed was soon discovered and he was forced to flee Egypt.

Moses walked and walked until he came to a place called Midian. There was a well there, and being thirsty, he stopped for a drink. Just then, the local priest's seven beautiful daughters came by to water their sheep. Unfortunately, some nasty shepherds arrived at the well. They tried to bully the women and scare them from the water, but Moses stepped in and defended the daughters. Their father was so grateful that he invited Moses to live with them. He even gave away one of his daughters to be Moses' wife.

A long time later, the Israelites were despondent and God heard their cries. Honoring the covenant made with Abraham and the Hebrews, God reached out to Moses. While tending to his flocks one day, Moses heard a voice coming from a bush. Now this was no ordinary bush! It was on fire, but was not burning up. The voice said, "Moses, I am the Lord God and I have heard the cries of your people in Egypt. You must go and set them free." Moses was aghast! "How can I do that? I am just a lowly shepherd and slow of speech with a damaged tongue." (Remember when Moses put that hot coal to his mouth?) "You will appear before Pharaoh as a God, with your brother Aaron as a prophet. He will do the speaking for you."

"He will do the speaking for you."
Exodus 4:16

Through Moses, God brought forth ten plagues on the people of Egypt.

God told Moses, "Throw down your staff!" Moses obeyed and his staff turned into a serpent. Then God said, "Pick it up by its tail." Moses was terrified, but did as he was told and the serpent turned back into a staff. The Lord said to Moses, "Have Aaron point his rod near Pharaoh's feet and I will bring serpents. If he is not sufficiently frightened, take some water from the Nile and pour it on the ground. Aaron will aim his rod at it, and the water will turn to blood. Pharaoh will consider freeing your people, but I will make him stubborn and uncaring so that he will still refuse to free them. Now go back to Egypt! When you get there, have Aaron execute the plan I have empowered you with."

Moses and Aaron traveled to Egypt and met with Pharaoh. When Aaron turned his staff into a serpent, the Pharaoh laughed and brought in his sorcerers to do the same thing! Quick as a wink, God's serpent ate the sorcerers' serpents. This made Pharaoh nervous and when Aaron turned the water into blood, this frightened Pharaoh. He briefly considered letting the Israelites go, but God did as promised and hardened his heart, so he would not let the people go. And so, Moses and Aaron left the palace.

The next day God said to Moses, "I have made Pharaoh stubborn and he refuses to let the people go. Have Aaron point his staff at the Nile and I will turn it into blood and all the fish shall die. In the vessels of wood and stone, that water too shall become blood." And it came to pass. The water turned to blood, and the Nile smelled horrible because the fish were dead. The people quickly became thirsty and terribly afraid. Unfazed by this plague of blood, Pharaoh summoned his sorcerers. With a spell, they were able to do the same thing, so Pharaoh, with a dismissive wave of his hand, left the courtyard and again did not free the slaves.

THE 10 PLAGUES

After seven days and seven nights,

Moses, instructed by God, said to Pharaoh, "Let my people go or the Lord will send a plague of frogs upon you. They will be in the rivers and streams, in your ovens and kneading bowls, and in your bed-chambers!" And so that too came to pass. There were frogs EVERYWHERE! But Pharaoh still would not let the people go.

"Have Aaron point his staff and I will bring a plague of lice throughout the land," said the Lord. Aaron pointed his staff and, indeed, God brought about the plague of lice. All the dust of the land became vermin. It was in the Egyptians' hair and clothes, on their animals and on the ground. When the Pharaoh's magicians tried to bring lice as the Lord did, they were unable to. Now, the Pharaoh was getting angry and upset, but (you guessed it), he didn't let any people go.

God brought down three more plagues;

flies, cattle-plague, and boils.

Pharaoh still wouldn't let the people go.

Now the Lord told Moses, "Go to Pharaoh and tell him this time I will hand down a monstrous hail. Everything out in the open will be pummeled to death and fire will rain between the hailstones." Since Pharaoh did not let the Israelites go, Moses held out his rod towards the heavens and down came the hail. Never before had the Egyptians witnessed such force. Along with the hail was thunder and lightning that made the trees catch fire and come crashing down. At this, the Pharaoh pleaded with Moses, "I stand guilty this time, your God is in the right, and I and my people are in the wrong. Please make it stop and I will let your people go free!" The Lord and Moses didn't really believe him, but God stopped the hail. Sure enough, as soon as the hail had stopped, Pharaoh changed his mind.

In a demonstration of awesome power and will, God brought three more plagues upon Egypt. God commanded Moses to raise his staff and the sky became dark with locusts. Anything that the hail and fire had not destroyed, the locusts consumed.

God saved the two most devastating plagues for last. Again, Moses held his staff high and emanated a darkness blacker than black into the air. It was so dark, you couldn't see your hand in front of your face. This darkness was so complete, candles were unable to light the way. Although it only lasted three days, it felt like a lifetime.

Then God told Moses, "Toward midnight, I will go forth among the Egyptians, and every firstborn in the land of Egypt shall die...and there shall be a loud cry in the land of Egypt, such as has never been, or will ever be again." (Ex.10:4-6)

At this point, the Pharaoh's advisors were begging him to give up and free the Israelite slaves. By this time, Pharaoh wanted to surrender and free the slaves, but God hardened his heart again to be sure he truly understood the awesome wrath that the Lord could bring down on Egypt.

God gave the Israelites instructions to keep them safe from the tenth plague, the killing of the firstborn. "Sacrifice an unblemished lamb this evening and use its blood to mark the door posts and lintels of your homes. Then eat it with unleavened bread and bitter herbs."

Around midnight, God brought forth the tenth and most devastating plague. In every Egyptian household, the firstborn child suddenly took ill and died. However, the plague "passed over" the homes of the Israelite slaves.

God has instructed us to take no pleasure in the suffering of the Egyptians. Although wine is a symbol of celebration, it is diminished as we reflect on their suffering. To commemorate each plague, we dip our little-finger into the wine, then place a drop on our plate while reciting the name of the plague.

The 10 Plagues

דָּם	**Blood**
צְפַרְדֵּעַ	**Frogs**
כִּנִּים	**Lice**
עָרוֹב	**Flies**
דֶּבֶר	**Cattle-Plague**
שְׁחִין	**Boils**
בָּרָד	**Hail**
אַרְבֶּה	**Locusts**
חֹשֶׁךְ	**Darkness**
מַכַּת בְּכוֹרוֹת	**Killing of the Firstborn**

"Let my people go!"

Knowing Pharaoh was not to be trusted, Moses told the Israelites to pack up whatever they could carry and head for the desert immediately. They carried food on their shoulders and brought grain to make bread. When they reached the desert, they made unleavened bread by baking the dough on hot rocks. Today we call this unleavened bread matzah.

The Israelites reached the Red Sea and were surrounded by Pharaoh's soldiers. Just when it looked like the Israelites were doomed, God instructed Moses, "Raise your staff toward the sea and I will send a mighty wind to part the waters." Moses raised the staff and the sea parted, allowing the Israelites to safely cross. Furious that they were getting away, the soldiers gave chase. Once the Israelites were safely across, Moses held up his staff and the sea closed upon Pharaoh's soldiers, drowning every one of them. Finally, the Israelites were truly free!

Go Down Moses pg. 40

"It would have been enough and we are grateful."

After each line is read, everyone present proclaims **Dayenu!**

Had God brought us out of Egypt, but not executed judgment against the Egyptians, it would have been enough.

Had God executed judgment against them, but not upon their gods, it would have been enough.

Had God executed judgment against their gods, but not slain their firstborn, it would have been enough.

Had God slain their firstborn, but not given us their wealth, it would have been enough.

Had God given us their wealth, but not split the Sea for us, it would have been enough.

Had God split the Sea for us, but not led us through it on dry land, it would have been enough.

Had God led us through it on dry land, but not drowned our oppressors in it, it would have been enough.

Had God drowned our oppressors in it, but not provided for our needs in the desert for forty years, it would have been enough.

Had God provided for our needs in the desert for forty years, but not fed us the Manna, it would have been enough.

Had God fed us the Manna, but not given us the Sabbath, it would have been enough.

Had God given us the Sabbath, but not brought us to Mount Sinai, it would have been enough.

Had God brought us to Mount Sinai, but not given us the Torah, it would have been enough.

Had God given us the Torah, but not brought us into the Land of Israel, it would have been enough.

Had God brought us into the Land of Israel, but not built us The Temple, it would have been enough.

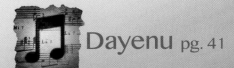
Dayenu pg. 41

We join together
to glorify and bless God

Leader: Dayenu reminds us that we should appreciate every moment in our lives. Let us be awestruck, and grateful for the many blessings we've received and let our hearts overflow with gratitude and appreciation.

Everyone: Amen

The matzot are covered. Raise your glass of wine and recite the following together:

We join together to glorify and bless God for bringing us out of slavery and bondage, for granting us our freedom, and for turning our sorrow into joy. We give thanks to God for helping us reach this night, so that we may celebrate the Seder by singing songs of praise for our redemption and freedom.

בָּרוּךְ אַתָּה יְיָ, אֱלֹהֵינוּ מֶלֶךְ הָעוֹלָם, בּוֹרֵא פְּרִי הַגָּפֶן:

Baruch Atah Adonai Eloheinu melech ha'olam borei p'ri hagafen.

Blessed are You, Adonai our God, Creator of the universe, Who creates the fruit of the vine.

Leader: Drink the second glass of wine while reclining, leaning to the left side. When your glass is empty, have the person sitting next to you refill it.

The Symbols of Passover

One of Judaism's greatest scholars, Rabban Gamliel, declared that the Seder is not complete unless we explain the meaning of the three main Passover symbols; Pesach, matzah and maror.

Point to the Pesach (roasted bone) and say:
This bone represents the mighty arm of God, that forced the Egyptians to free the slaves. It also represents the Paschal lamb that was offered as a special sacrifice in the days of the ancient Temple in Jerusalem.

Point to the matzah and say:
This is the bread of affliction that our ancestors ate in the land of Egypt.

Point to the maror and say:
This maror reminds us of the bitter lives we endured as slaves to the Pharaoh.

Part 6
Rachtzah 2nd Hand Washing

Everyone:
Blessed are You, Adonai our God, Creator of the universe, Who has made us holy by Your mitzvot and commands us to wash our hands.
Wash hands

Part 7
Motzi Blessing Over Bread

Leader: **instruction:** Lift the matzah plate and recite the following prayer:

בָּרוּךְ אַתָּה יְיָ, אֱלֹהֵינוּ מֶלֶךְ הָעוֹלָם, הַמּוֹצִיא לֶחֶם מִן הָאָרֶץ:

Baruch Atah Adonai Eloheinu melech ha'olam hamotzi lechem min ha'aretz.

Blessed are You, Adonai our God, Creator of the universe, Who brings forth bread from the earth.

Part 8
Matzah Blessing Over Matzah

Leader: **instruction:** give each participant a piece of matzah taken from one of the top two matzot and recite the following:

In the Torah God commands, "Seven days you shall eat unleavened bread." Matzah symbolizes the unleavened bread our ancestors ate while fleeing Egypt. Because they did not have time to allow the dough to rise, they were forced to bake their dough before it leavened, and eat it in the form of hard, flat, crackers, which we call matzah.

Everyone:

בָּרוּךְ אַתָּה יְיָ, אֱלֹהֵינוּ מֶלֶךְ הָעוֹלָם, אֲשֶׁר קִדְּשָׁנוּ בְּמִצְוֹתָיו וְצִוָּנוּ עַל אֲכִילַת מַצָּה:

Baruch Atah Adonai Eloheinu melech ha'olam asher kid'shanu b'mitzvotav v'tzivanu al achilat matzah.

Blessed are You, Adonai our God, Creator of the universe, Who makes us holy with Your commandments, and has given us the mitzvah of eating matzah.

Eat the matzah while reclining, leaning to the left side.

"Freed by the mighty hand of God!"

Part 9
Maror Blessing over Bitter Herbs

Participant: Maror symbolizes the bitter life of slavery, while charoset represents the mortar used by the Jewish slaves to build the Pharaoh's cities. Each generation must regard themselves as if slaves to Pharaoh and freed by the mighty hand of God!

Everyone: Dip the maror into the charoset and recite the following blessing:

בָּרוּךְ אַתָּה יְיָ, אֱלֹהֵינוּ מֶלֶךְ הָעוֹלָם, אֲשֶׁר קִדְּשָׁנוּ בְּמִצְוֹתָיו וְצִוָּנוּ עַל אֲכִילַת מָרוֹר:

Baruch Atah Adonai Eloheinu melech ha'olam asher kid'shanu b'mitzvotav v'tzivanu al achilat maror.

Blessed are You, Adonai our God, Creator of the universe, Who makes us holy with Your mitzvot, and has given us the mitzvah of eating maror.

Eat the maror and charoset together.

Part 10
Korech   Hillel's Sandwich

Participant: In the days of the Second Temple in Jerusalem, around 75 B.C.E., Rabbi Hillel used to make a sandwich with Pesach (sacrificial lamb), matzah, and maror. These ingredients were eaten together to satisfy the commandment of eating the Pesach with matzah and bitter herbs. Since we no longer offer sacrifices, no lamb is used.

Using the bottom matzah, we make a sandwich of matzah and maror (or chazeret). Charoset may be added to the sandwich as long as the bitter taste is still present.

Eat the sandwich and...

Part 11
Shulchan Orech   When do we eat?

The Seder plate is now removed and each participant is given a hard-boiled egg (peeled).

Participant: It's customary to eat hard-boiled eggs as part of the Seder. Passover is a spring festival, and we now take an egg, dip it in salt water and eat it as a symbol of springtime and rebirth.

The festive Passover meal is now served!

Part 12
Tzafun Afikoman

After dinner, when the Afikoman is found and presented, it is shared and eaten as the final dessert. This reminds us of how sweet freedom is compared to slavery.

Part 13
Barech Blessing after the meal / Birkat Hamazon

Participant: Blessed are You, Adonai our God, Creator of the universe, Who makes us holy with Your commandment to honor Pesach, and Who in goodness, mercy, and kindness has provided us food for this festive meal.

Everyone:

May the Holy One who creates peace in the heavens, grant peace for us and all Israel... Amen.

Participant:

Blessed are you, Lord our God, Creator of the universe, who nourishes the world with grace, kindness and mercy. You give food to all creatures, for Your kindness endures forever. Through Your great goodness, may we never be in want of sustenance. You are the God who sustains all, does good to all, and provides food for all the creatures which You have created. Blessed are you, O Lord, who sustains all.

Wine Blessing 3rd glass

Everyone: **instruction:** Fill the wine glass of the person sitting next to you, then recite the following blessing:

בָּרוּךְ אַתָּה יְיָ, אֱלֹהֵינוּ מֶלֶךְ הָעוֹלָם, בּוֹרֵא פְּרִי הַגָּפֶן:

Baruch Atah Adonai Eloheinu melech ha'olam borei p'ri hagafen.

Blessed are You, Adonai our God, Creator of the universe,
Who creates the fruit of the vine.

Drink; then have your fourth glass of wine filled by the person next to you.

We Welcome Elijah

Leader: **instruction:** Fill Elijah's cup with wine and say:

Enter Elijah. Are we worthy as a people, worthy enough for you to present yourself to us? Are we holy enough to share this Passover Seder with you, Oh Elijah the prophet? If so, please enter and let us welcome you!

Open the door for Elijah.

If Elijah does not enter, all say the following prayer:
Someday, the prophet Elijah will return to earth and lead us to an age of peace. We pray this day will come soon.

Close the door.

Eliyahu Ha-Navi pg. 41

35

Miriam's Cup optional

Leader: **instruction:**

Fill Miriam's cup with water and say...

We place a cup on our Seder table to remind us of Miriam's well, which provided everlasting, sustaining water for us and our animals while we wandered in the desert. This cup also represents the many Jewish women who have made a positive difference to the Jewish people.

Part 14

Hallel Praise God

Participant: The word Halleluyah comes from combining the Hebrew word hallelu, meaning "praise," and the word Yah meaning "God." Thus, we have Halleluyah, meaning "praise God."

We recite the following prayer together:
Give thanks to God, all nations and peoples; praise the Lord!

For God's kindness overwhelms us, and the truth and love of the Holy One is great and forever.

Halleluyah!

Halleluyah!

Counting of the Omer
2nd night only

"...and you shall count off seven weeks and one day,

50 DAYS

then you shall bring an offering of new grain to the Lord..."

Leviticus 23:16

Participant: Our ancestors used to bring a sheaf of barley from their first fall harvest, as an offering to the Temple in Jerusalem. We commemorate this by counting the seven week period from the second night of Passover to the day before Shavuot, known as...

"The Days of the Omer."

Since this is the second night of Passover, we say the following prayer and begin the count:

בָּרוּךְ אַתָּה יְיָ, אֱלֹהֵינוּ מֶלֶךְ הָעוֹלָם, אֲשֶׁר קִדְּשָׁנוּ בְּמִצְוֹתָיו וְצִוָּנוּ עַל סְפִירַת הָעוֹמֶר:

Baruch Atah Adonai Eloheinu melech ha'olam asher kid'shanu b'mitzvotav v'tzivanu al sefirat ha'omer.

Blessed are You, Adonai our God, Creator of the Universe, who makes us holy, and gives us the mitzvah of counting the Omer.

As we count the Omer, so may we learn to appreciate every day as a blessing and a gift as we look forward with excitement and anticipation to receiving the Torah at Shavuot.

Amen!

> ❝Thou who dwellest on high...
> bring the redeemed to Zion, with joyful song.❞
>
> Prague Haggadah circa 1526

Wine Blessing (fourth glass)

Everyone: Raise the fourth glass of wine and say:

בָּרוּךְ אַתָּה יְיָ, אֱלֹהֵינוּ מֶלֶךְ הָעוֹלָם, בּוֹרֵא פְּרִי הַגָּפֶן:

Baruch Atah Adonai Eloheinu melech ha'olam borei p'ri hagafen.

Blessed are You, Adonai our God, Creator of the universe, Who creates the fruit of the vine.

Drink the fourth and final glass of wine.

Leader: **Our Seder is now concluded. All present say:**

לְשָׁנָה הַבָּאָה בִּירוּשָׁלָיִם:

"L'Shana Ha'ba-a B'Yerushalayim!"

"Next Year...
in Jerusalem!"

 Who Knows One?   Chad Gadya   Adir Hu   pgs. 42-45

Seder songs

Go Down Moses - Let My People Go!

When Israel was in Egypt land,
Let my people go.

Oppressed so hard they could not stand,
Let my people go.

Go down, Moses, way down in Egypt land,
Tell ol' Pharaoh, let my people go.

Thus saith the Lord, bold Moses said,
Let my people go.

If not I'll smite your people dead,
Let my people go.

Go down, Moses, way down in Egypt land,
Tell ol' Pharaoh, let my people go.

As Israel stood by the water side,
Let my people go.

By God's command it did divide,
Let my people go.

Go down, Moses, way down in Egypt land,
Tell ol' Pharaoh, let my people go.

turn back to page 27

Dayenu!

Ilu hotsi, hotsianu,
hotsianu mimitsrayim,
hotsianu mimitsrayim,
Dayenu!

Da, dayenu! (3X)
Dayenu! Dayenu!

Ilu natan, natan lanu,
natan lanu et hatorah,
natan lanu et hatorah,
Dayenu!

Da, dayenu! (3X)
Dayenu! Dayenu!

Ilu natan, natan lanu,
natan lanu et hashabbat,
natan lanu et hashabbat,
Dayenu!

Da, dayenu! (3X)
Dayenu! Dayenu!

turn back to page 29

Eliyahu Ha-Navi
Elijah, the Prophet

Eliyahu ha-Navi, Eliyahu ha-Tishbi, Eliyahu, Eliyahu, Eliyahu ha-Giladi.
Bimhayrah v'yamenu, yavo aleynu, im Moshiach ben David, im Moshiach ben David.
Elijah the Prophet, Elijah the Tishbite, Elijah, Elijah, Elijah the Giladite.
Speedily and in our days, come to us, with the Messiah, son of David,
with the Messiah, son of David.

turn back to page 35

WHO knows one?

Echad Mi Yodea

Try singing using only one breath per verse.

1 who knows 1?
1 I know 1
1 is Our God who is in the heavens and on earth

2 who knows 2?
2 I know 2
2 are the tablets of the commandments
1 is Our God who is in the heavens and on earth

3 who knows 3?
3 I know 3
3 are our patriarchs
2 are the tablets of the commandments
1 is Our God who is in the heavens and on earth

4 who knows 4?
4 I know 4
4 are our matriarchs
3 are our patriarchs
2 are the tablets of the commandments
1 is Our God who is in the heavens and on earth

5 who knows 5?
5 I know 5
5 are the books of the Torah
4 are our matriarchs
3 are our patriarchs
2 are the tablets of the commandments
1 is Our God who is in the heavens and on earth

6 who knows 6?
6 I know 6
6 are the orders of the Mishnah
5 are the books of the Torah
4 are our matriarchs
3 are our patriarchs
2 are the tablets of the commandments
1 is Our God who is in the heavens and on earth

7 who knows 7?
7 I know 7
7 are the days in a week
6 are the orders of the Mishnah
5 are the books of the Torah
4 are our matriarchs
3 are our patriarchs
2 are the tablets of the commandments
1 is Our God who is in the heavens and on earth

8 who knows 8?
8 I know 8
8 are the days to the brit milah
7 are the days in a week
6 are the orders of the Mishnah
5 are the books of the Torah
4 are our matriarchs
3 are our patriarchs
2 are the tablets of the commandments
1 is Our God who is in the heavens and on earth

9 who knows 9?
9 I know 9
9 are the months before birth
8 are the days to the brit milah
7 are the days in a week
6 are the orders of the Mishnah
5 are the books of the Torah
4 are our matriarchs
3 are our patriarchs
2 are the tablets of the commandments
1 is Our God who is in the heavens and on earth

10 who knows 10?
10 I know 10
10 are the commandments
9 are the months before birth
8 are the days to the brit milah
7 are the days in a week
6 are the orders of the Mishnah
5 are the books of the Torah
4 are our matriarchs
3 are our patriarchs
2 are the tablets of the commandments
1 is Our God who is in the heavens and on earth

11 who knows 11?
11 I know 11
11 are the stars in Joseph's dream
10 are the commandments
9 are the months before birth
8 are the days to the brit milah
7 are the days in a week
6 are the orders of the Mishnah
5 are the books of the Torah
4 are our matriarchs
3 are our patriarchs
2 are the tablets of the commandments
1 is Our God who is in the heavens and on earth

12 who knows 12?
12 I know 12
12 are the Tribes of Israel
11 are the stars in Joseph's dream
10 are the commandments
9 are the months before birth
8 are the days to the brit milah
7 are the days in a week
6 are the orders of the Mishnah
5 are the books of the Torah
4 are our matriarchs
3 are our patriarchs
2 are the tablets of the commandments
1 is Our God who is in the heavens and on earth

Chad Gadya

Note: "Two zuzim" is an amount of money. A "kid" is a baby goat.

Chad gadya, chad gadya.
My father bought a kid for two zuzim.
Chad gadya, chad gadya.

Then came the cat that ate the kid,
My father bought for two zuzim.
Chad gadya, chad gadya.

Then came the dog that bit the cat,
that ate the kid,
My father bought for two zuzim.
Chad gadya, chad gadya.

Then came the stick that beat the dog,
that bit the cat that ate the kid,
My father bought for two zuzim.
Chad gadya, chad gadya.

Then came the fire that burned the stick,
that beat the dog that bit the cat,
that ate the kid,
My father bought for two zuzim.
Chad gadya, chad gadya.

Then came the water that quenched the fire,
that burned the stick that beat the dog,
that bit the cat that ate the kid,
My father bought for two zuzim.
Chad gadya, chad gadya.

Then came the ox that drank the water,
that quenched the fire that burned the stick,
that beat the dog that bit the cat,
that ate the kid,
My father bought for two zuzim.
Chad gadya, chad gadya.

Then came the butcher that slew the ox,
that drank the water that quenched the fire,
that burned the stick that beat the dog,
that bit the cat that ate the kid,
My father bought for two zuzim.
Chad gadya, chad gadya.

Then came the angel of death,
that killed the butcher that slew the ox,
that drank the water that quenched the fire,
that burned the stick that beat the dog,
that bit the cat that ate the kid,
My father bought for two zuzim.
Chad gadya, chad gadya.

Then came the Holy One, blessed be God!
Who destroyed the Angel of death,
that killed the butcher that slew the ox,
that drank the water that quenched the fire,
that burned the stick that beat the dog,
that bit the cat that ate the kid,
My father bought for two zuzim.
Chad gadya, chad gadya.

Adir Hu

Adir hu, adir hu...

Yivneh veito bekarov, bimheirah, bimheirah, beyameinu beka'rov.

Ehl benei, Ehl benei

Benei veit-cha beka'arov.

Bachur hu, gadol hu, dagul hu.

Yivneh veito bekarov, bimheirah, bimheirah, beyameinu beka'rov.

Hadur hu, vatik hu, zakai hu.

Yivneh veito bekarov, bimheirah, bimheirah, beyameinu beka'rov.

Chassid hu, tahor hu, yachid hu.

Yivneh veito bekarov, bimheirah, bimheirah, beyameinu beka'rov.

Kabir hu, lamud hu, melech hu.

Yivneh veito bekarov, bimheirah, bimheirah, beyameinu beka'rov.

Nora hu, sagiv hu, izuz hu.

Yivneh veito bekarov, bimheirah, bimheirah, beyameinu beka'rov.

Podeh hu, tzadik hu, kadosh hu.

Yivneh veito bekarov, bimheirah, bimheirah, beyameinu beka'rov.

Rachum hu, shaddai hu, takif hu.

Yivneh veito bekarov, bimheirah, bimheirah, beyameinu beka'rov.

Ehl benei, Ehl benei

Benei veit-cha beka'arov!